Path
to
Seven
Figures

Wealth Strategies

Path to Seven Figures

Wealth Strategies

The roadmap to financial freedom

Richard Green

Cover design by Ropdi Designs
Cover background and internal page opener images by Ropdi Designs
Internal design and figures by Pixel Inspirations

Disclaimer
The content in this publication is a form of general commentary and should not be construed as professional advice. It is not meant to offer specific guidance for individual situations, and individuals should not depend on it as the sole basis for making decisions to take or abstain from any actions discussed within. Before making any such decisions, readers are advised to seek professional guidance where appropriate. The author disclaims all responsibility and liability, to the fullest extent permitted by law, for any consequences arising directly or indirectly from individuals taking or refraining from action based on the information provided in this publication. Please note that this publication may not contain the most current information available.

Contents

Acknowledgements

I extend my deepest gratitude to my father for his profound wisdom that has guided the creation of "Path to Seven Figures Wealth Strategies."

To my mentors, advisors, family, and friends, your unwavering support has been instrumental in this journey.

And to the readers, may this book inspire and empower you on your path to financial success.

Thank you all for being part of this incredible voyage.in my abilities have fuelled my determination and propelled me toward success.

About the author

Richard Green is a seasoned financial expert and entrepreneur dedicated to empowering individuals on their journey to financial success. With a wealth of experience in entrepreneurship, investing, and personal finance, Richi has spent years studying and mastering the principles of wealth creation and abundance.

Drawing inspiration from luminaries and mentors, Richi has distilled their knowledge and insights into a comprehensive guide that offers practical strategies and actionable advice for achieving seven-figure wealth. Through their writing, Richi seeks to inspire and empower readers to take control of their financial destiny, guiding them along the path to prosperity with wisdom, clarity, and unwavering determination.

With a passion for helping others achieve their financial goals, Richi brings a unique blend of expertise, empathy, and enthusiasm to his work. Whether through books, seminars, or one-on-one coaching, Richi is committed to sharing his knowledge and insights to help individuals unlock their full potential and create a life of abundance and fulfilment.

"Building wealth, building communities"

How to use this book

As you embark on this transformative journey toward financial abundance and prosperity, it's essential to understand how to navigate the treasures that lie within these pages. Here's how to make the most of your exploration:

Set Your Course

Begin by setting clear intentions and goals for your journey. Define what achieving seven-figure wealth means to you and why it's important. Use the insights and strategies in this book to chart a course that aligns with your aspirations and values.

Absorb the Wisdom

Dive deep into each chapter. Take the time to absorb the principles and strategies presented, reflecting on how they apply to your own financial journey.

Take Action

Knowledge alone is not enough – it's the actions you take that will propel you toward your goals. As you read each chapter, identify actionable steps you can take to implement the strategies and principles discussed. Whether it's starting a business, investing in stocks, or creating a budget, take decisive action to move closer to seven-figure wealth.

Stay Open-Minded

Keep an open mind as you explore new ideas and concepts. Be willing to challenge your existing beliefs and assumptions about money and wealth.

Remember that growth and success often require stepping outside your comfort zone and embracing new ways of thinking and doing.

Seek Guidance

Don't hesitate to seek guidance and support along the way. Whether it's from mentors, advisors, or fellow readers, surround yourself with people who can offer valuable insights and encouragement. Share your experiences and insights with others and learn from their successes and challenges.

Persist and Persevere

The journey to seven-figure wealth is not always easy, but it is worth it. Stay committed to your goals, and don't let setbacks or obstacles deter you from your path. Stay focused, stay determined, and keep moving forward, knowing that every step you take brings you closer to your destination.

Celebrate Your Progress

Along the way, take time to celebrate your achievements and milestones. Whether it's reaching a financial goal, achieving a personal milestone, or overcoming a challenge, celebrate your progress and acknowledge how far you've come. Use these moments of celebration as fuel to propel you forward on your journey to seven-figure wealth.

May your journey along the "Path to Seven Figures Wealth Strategies" be filled with abundance, prosperity, and the fulfilment of your deepest desires.

Chapter 1
Setting Your Financial Goals

Welcome, fellow seekers of financial wisdom!

In this chapter, we embark on a journey that will transform your relationship with money and pave the way for a future of abundance and prosperity. We're diving deep into the crucial first step: setting your financial goals.

Picture this

You're standing on the shore, gazing out at the vast ocean of opportunity. But without a map, without a destination in mind, you're simply adrift, at the mercy of the currents. That's where setting your financial goals comes in – it's your compass, guiding you towards the shores of financial freedom.

Now, let me share a little anecdote from my own journey. Back when I was struggling financially, I realized that I was like a ship without a rudder, tossed about by the waves of circumstance. It wasn't until I sat down and clarified my financial goals that I began to chart a course towards success.

So, my friend, grab a seat, pour yourself a cup of coffee, and let's delve into the art of setting financial goals.

Dream Big, Start Small: Close your eyes and envision your ideal financial future. What does it look like? Take a moment to dream without limits. Do you see yourself living in a beautiful home, driving your dream car, or travelling the world? Whatever it is, jot it down. Remember, the size of your dreams determines the magnitude of your success.

Be Specific, Be Realistic: Now that you've painted a picture of your dreams, it's time to add some detail. How much money do you need to make those dreams a reality? Break it down into tangible, achievable goals.

Whether it's paying off debt, saving for a down payment on a house, or building a retirement nest egg, get specific. And remember, while it's important to dream big, it's equally important to be realistic.

Short-Term vs. Long-Term Goals

Think of your financial goals as a series of checkpoints on your journey. Start by setting short-term goals – things you want to achieve in the next year or two. These could be as simple as setting up an emergency fund or paying off high-interest debt. Then, set your sights on the long-term – the big-ticket items that might take five, ten, or even twenty years to achieve. Whether it's owning a home, starting a business, or retiring comfortably, break it down into manageable milestones.

SMART Goals Rule

You've probably heard of SMART goals – Specific, Measurable, Achievable, Relevant, and Time-bound. And let me tell you, they're the secret sauce to goal-setting success. Your financial goals should tick all these boxes. Instead of saying, "I want to be rich," say, "I want to have $1 million in my retirement account by the time I'm 50." See the difference? It's all about clarity and precision.

Put Pen to Paper, Review Regularly

The act of writing down your goals is like planting seeds in fertile soil – it gives them roots; it gives them life. So, grab a notebook or fire up your favourite note-taking app and start jotting down your financial goals. Then, put them somewhere you'll see them every day – on your fridge, your desk, or your bathroom mirror.

And don't forget to review them regularly. Life is fluid, my friend, and so are your goals. It's okay to adjust them as you grow and evolve.

Setting your financial goals is not just a one-time exercise – it's an ongoing process that requires dedication and intentionality. But trust me when I say this: it's worth every ounce of effort. So, take the time to dream big, to get specific, and to map out your path to financial freedom. Your future self will thank you for it.

Chapter 2
Understanding Your
Current Financial Situation

In this chapter, we're embarking on a thrilling expedition through the labyrinth of your current financial situation – a crucial stage in our quest for wealth mastery.

Picture this

You're an explorer setting out on a grand adventure, but before you can conquer new territories, you must first map out your starting point. Likewise, understanding your current financial situation serves as your compass, guiding you through the twists and turns of the financial landscape.

Allow me to share a personal anecdote from my own journey. There was a time when I thought I had a firm grasp on my finances, but upon closer inspection, I discovered hidden complexities and overlooked opportunities. It was like peeling back the layers of an onion – each revelation bringing me closer to the core of financial clarity.

So, dear reader, grab a seat, pour yourself a cup of ambition, and let's embark on this exhilarating voyage through the realm of your finances.

Illuminate Your Assets

The first step in unravelling your financial tapestry is to take stock of your assets – those precious resources that contribute to your net worth. Make a comprehensive list, including your savings accounts, investments, real estate holdings, and any other valuable possessions. Think of it as shining a spotlight on the treasures hidden within your financial fortress.

Navigate Your Liabilities

Next, we must confront the shadowy underworld of liabilities – those debts and obligations that threaten to weigh us down. Catalogue your liabilities with meticulous detail, from credit card balances to outstanding loans. By shedding light on these lurking debts, we can devise strategies to vanquish them and reclaim our financial sovereignty.

Chart Your Cash Flow

Now, let's turn our attention to the ebb and flow of your financial river – your income and expenses. Track every incoming stream of revenue, from your primary salary to supplementary sources of income. Then, scrutinize your expenditures with eagle-eyed precision, distinguishing between essential necessities and discretionary indulgences. This voyage of self-discovery will reveal the currents that shape your financial tides.

Interrogate Your Financial Habits

With a clearer understanding of your cash flow, it's time to interrogate your financial habits. Are you a wise steward of your resources, or do you squander them frivolously? Do you possess the discipline to save and invest for the future, or do you succumb to the siren song of instant gratification? By confronting these habits head-on, we can unearth the seeds of financial success or identify areas for improvement.

Evaluate Your Financial Vital Signs

Armed with this newfound knowledge, it's time to assess the vital signs of your financial health. Calculate your debt-to-income ratio, an indicator of your debt burden relative to your earnings. Scrutinise your credit score, a barometer of your financial reputation in the eyes of lenders. And examine the robustness of your emergency fund, a safeguard against unforeseen tempests. By evaluating these critical metrics, we gain insight into our financial fortitude and identify areas ripe for fortification.

Envision Your Financial Horizon

Finally, let us cast our gaze toward the shimmering shores of our financial horizon. Armed with a comprehensive understanding of our current financial situation, we can chart a course toward our desired destination.

What dreams beckon on the distant horizon? Is it a debt-free existence, a comfortable retirement, or the pursuit of entrepreneurial endeavours? Whatever your aspirations, articulate them with clarity and conviction, for they shall serve as the guiding stars on our voyage to wealth mastery.

Understanding your current financial situation is akin to wielding a compass in the uncharted waters of financial uncertainty – it empowers you to navigate the turbulent seas with confidence and purpose. So, embrace this journey of self-discovery, for it is the first step toward unlocking the boundless treasures that await you on the road to riches.

Chapter 3
Creating a Budget That Works

Today, we embark on a thrilling expedition into the heart of financial management – the creation of a budget that not only guides your spending but propels you toward your dreams. So, grab your compass, fasten your seatbelt, and let's navigate the twists and turns of budget creation together.

Set Sail with Clear Intentions

You're the captain of your financial ship, charting a course toward the shores of prosperity. But before you can set sail, you must first plot your destination. What are your financial goals? Do you dream of owning a home, travelling the world, or achieving financial independence? Whatever your aspirations, let them be your guiding star as you set sail on the seas of budget creation.

Hoist Your Income Anchors

Your income is the wind in your financial sails, propelling you toward your goals. Take stock of all your income sources, from your main salary to any side hustles or passive income streams. Be thorough in your tallying, for every doubloon earned is a treasure to be cherished.

Navigate the Expenses Reef

Beware, for hidden dangers lurk beneath the surface of your financial ocean – the dreaded expenses reef. Dive deep into your expenditures, categorizing them into essentials like housing, transportation, and groceries, and discretionary spending like dining out and entertainment. But beware, me hearties, for even the smallest leak in your budget can sink your financial ship.

Trim the Financial Fat

As you navigate the treacherous waters of your expenses, be on the lookout for financial fat that weighs down your budget. Distinguish between needs and wants, cutting back on frivolous spending to trim your financial sails and increase your speed toward your financial destination.

Plot Your Course with Realistic Limits

Now that you've mapped out the terrain of your income and expenses, it's time to plot your course with realistic limits for each spending category. Be mindful of your financial goals and allocate your resources, accordingly, setting a steady course toward financial freedom.

Stay the Course and Adjust Your Sails

As you sail toward your financial horizon, be prepared to adjust your sails to the winds of change. Regularly monitor your spending against your budgeted amounts, making course corrections as needed to stay on track toward your goals. And remember, flexibility is the key to weathering any financial storm that may come your way.

Celebrate Every Victory

Hoist the Jolly Roger and break out the grog, for every victory on your financial journey is cause for celebration! Whether it's paying off debt, reaching a savings milestone, or sticking to your budget for a month straight, take a moment to raise a toast to your financial success and revel in the joy of progress.

Crafting a budget that works is not just about crunching numbers – it's about navigating the high seas of financial management with courage, determination, and a sense of adventure.

Chapter 4
Developing Multiple Income Streams

In this chapter, we're delving deep into the riches that await those who dare to cultivate multiple income streams – a veritable treasure trove of opportunities to fortify your financial fortress and sail toward the shores of true prosperity. So, grab your compass, unfurl your sails, and let's embark on this exhilarating journey together.

The Symphony of Income: You're the conductor of your own financial orchestra, orchestrating a symphony of income streams that harmonize to create a melody of wealth. But instead of relying on a single instrument to carry the tune, you harness the power of multiple instruments to create a symphony of abundance. That's the magic of multiple income streams – it's like composing a masterpiece with a multitude of notes.

Casting Your Net Wide

The first step in unlocking the wealth of multiple income streams is to cast your net wide and identify the diverse sources of revenue available to you. These could include your primary job, freelance gigs, rental properties, dividends from investments, royalties from intellectual property, affiliate marketing, and more. By diversifying your income sources, you not only spread your risk but also open yourself up to a world of untapped potential.

Sailing with Your Strengths

As you navigate the seas of multiple income streams, it's essential to sail with the wind at your back by leveraging your unique strengths, skills, and passions. Are you a gifted writer, artist, or musician? Consider monetizing your creativity through freelance work, selling your art, or licensing your music. Do you have a knack for teaching, coaching, or consulting? Offer your expertise to others in exchange for a fee. By capitalizing on your strengths, you can turn your passions into profits and set sail toward financial success.

Exploring New Horizons

Don't be afraid to chart a course toward new horizons and explore uncharted waters in search of additional income streams. Keep an eye out for emerging trends, new technologies, and untapped markets that offer opportunities for growth. Whether it's starting a side hustle, launching an online business, or investing in real estate, be open to new possibilities and embrace the spirit of adventure. After all, fortune favours the bold!

The Power of Passive Income

One of the most potent forms of income is passive income – money that flows into your coffers with minimal effort or ongoing maintenance. This could include rental income from investment properties, dividends from stocks, royalties from books or music, affiliate marketing commissions, and more. By building passive income streams, you can create a steady flow of revenue that continues to grow over time, even when you're not actively working. It's like planting seeds that bear fruit year after year, allowing you to reap the rewards of your labour for generations to come.

Navigating the Waters of Time and Resources

As you navigate the seas of multiple income streams, it's crucial to manage your time and resources wisely. Prioritize your activities based on their potential for income generation and focus on high-impact tasks that yield the greatest return on investment. Delegate or automate routine tasks whenever possible to free up your time for more profitable pursuits. Remember, time is your most precious resource – spend it wisely.

Adapting to the Winds of Change

The winds of change are ever shifting, and it's essential to stay nimble and adapt to new challenges and opportunities as they arise. Keep a weather eye on the horizon, monitor your income streams closely, and be prepared to adjust your course as needed to stay on track toward your financial goals. By remaining flexible and responsive to change, you can navigate the turbulent waters of the financial markets with confidence and resilience.

Developing multiple income streams is not just about padding your bank account – it's about building a resilient financial portfolio that can weather any storm and provide you with the freedom and flexibility to live life on your terms. So, hoist your sails, seize the day, and let the winds of opportunity carry you toward your dreams.

Chapter 5
Investing Basics:
Stocks, Bonds, and Real Estate

In this chapter, we're diving deep into the world of investment – a thrilling voyage through the seas of stocks, bonds, and real estate. Join me aboard our financial vessel as we navigate the waves of opportunity and uncover the treasures that await those with the courage to set sail.

Stocks: The Ocean of Equities

You're a captain navigating the vast ocean of equities, each stock a ship carrying the hopes and dreams of its investors. Investing in stocks means owning a piece of a company – a share in its profits, losses, and future growth. While stocks can be volatile, they offer the potential for high returns and are an essential part of any well-rounded investment portfolio. But beware, me hearties – navigating the seas of stocks requires careful research, diversification, and a steady hand at the helm.

Bonds: Anchoring Your Portfolio

Bonds are like sturdy anchors that keep your portfolio steady in the face of market turbulence. When you invest in bonds, you're lending money to governments or corporations in exchange for regular interest payments and the return of your principal at maturity. Bonds offer a reliable source of income and can help cushion your portfolio against stock market fluctuations. While they may not offer the same potential for growth as stocks, bonds provide stability and security – like a safe harbour in a storm.

Real Estate: Building Your Financial Empire

Real estate is the treasure island of investing – a tangible asset that can provide both income and appreciation over time. Whether it's rental properties, commercial buildings, or vacant land, real estate offers a wealth of opportunities for savvy investors. From passive rental income to property appreciation, real estate can be a powerful wealth-building tool when approached with careful planning and strategy. But like any adventure, investing in real estate requires knowledge, patience, and a willingness to roll up your sleeves and get your hands dirty.

Diversification

Spreading Your Wealth Across the Seven Seas: One of the cardinal rules of investing is diversification – the practice of spreading your investments across different asset classes to reduce risk and maximize returns. By diversifying your portfolio with a mix of stocks, bonds, and real estate, you can weather the ups and downs of the market and increase your chances of long-term success. Remember, don't put all your treasure in one chest – spread your wealth across multiple investments to protect yourself against unforeseen dangers.

Research and Due Diligence

Charting When it comes to investing, knowledge is your most valuable treasure. Take the time to research and understand the investments you're considering, from the fundamentals of individual companies to the macroeconomic trends shaping the market as a whole. By arming yourself with knowledge and exercising due diligence, you can navigate the seas of investment with confidence and skill.

Patience and Discipline

The journey of investing is not for the faint of heart – it requires patience, discipline, and a steady hand on the tiller. The financial markets can be turbulent and unpredictable at times, but with patience and discipline, you can navigate through even the roughest waters. Stay focused on your long-term goals, resist the temptation to react impulsively to market fluctuations, and maintain a steady course toward financial freedom. Remember, investing is a marathon, not a sprint – so stay the course and trust in the power of time and compounding to grow your wealth over time. Investing in stocks, bonds, and real estate is not just about making money – it's about building a financial legacy that can last for generations. So, hoist your sails, set your course, and let the winds of investment carry you toward your dreams.

Chapter 6
Building a Solid Emergency Fund

In this chapter, we embark on a voyage into the vital realm of building a robust emergency fund – an essential bulwark against life's tempests and a beacon of stability in uncertain times. So, gather 'round, my friends, and let us delve into the importance of fortifying your financial fortress with an ample emergency fund.

The Bedrock of Financial Stability

Imagine, if you will, that you're the captain of your financial ship, navigating the vast seas of economic uncertainty. Just as a sturdy hull keeps a ship afloat in stormy waters, your emergency fund serves as the bedrock of your financial stability. It cushions you against unexpected squalls – whether they be a sudden job loss, a medical emergency, or an unforeseen repair bill – ensuring that your ship remains steady amidst the waves.

The Threefold Shield

When it comes to building an emergency fund, heed the wisdom of the ages and embrace the rule of three. Aim to stash away three to six months' worth of living expenses – a treasure trove that will see you through the darkest of financial storms. While the task may seem daunting, remember that every piece of gold buried in your chest brings you one step closer to true financial security. So, set your sights on the horizon and chart your course with determination and resolve.

Embark with a Single Step

The journey to building an emergency fund begins with a single step. Start small by setting aside a portion of your earnings each month – even if it be but a modest sum. As you grow accustomed to saving, gradually increase your contributions until you reach your target goal. And don't be afraid to dream big – envision the peace of mind that comes with having a fully-funded emergency fund, and let that vision propel you forward on your quest.

Harness the Power of Automation

Make use of modern marvels to ease the burden of saving for emergencies. Set up automatic transfers from your checking account to a dedicated savings vessel, ensuring that a portion of your plunder is stashed away before you're tempted to spend it. Automating your savings not only streamlines the process but also instils discipline in your financial habits, ensuring that your treasure chest grows steadily over time.

Trim Sails and Seek Treasure

As you sail toward the shores of financial security, trim unnecessary expenses from your budget and seek out new sources of treasure to bolster your emergency fund. Cut back on non-essential expenditures, such as dining out or entertainment, and redirect those doubloons into your savings chest. And don't forget to explore opportunities to increase your income – whether through a side hustle, freelancing, or investing in your skills and education. Every extra piece of gold you save or earn brings you one step closer to true financial freedom.

Stay the Course, Come What May

Building an emergency fund requires patience, perseverance, and a steadfast commitment to your financial goals. Stay the course, even when the winds of life grow turbulent, and trust in the power of consistency and determination to see you through. Every small victory along the way – every additional piece of treasure tucked away in your chest – brings you closer to the peace of mind and security you seek.

As you journey toward the shores of financial security, know that your emergency fund stands as a beacon of hope in troubled waters. With every piece of treasure, you add to your chest, you're building a sanctuary of stability that will shield you and your loved ones from life's storms. So, batten down the hatches, stay the course, and let the winds of financial freedom carry you toward a brighter future.

Chapter 7
Eliminating Debt:
Strategies for Debt Reduction

In this chapter, we're embarking on a daring quest to slay the mighty debt dragon and seize control of our financial destiny. Join me as we arm ourselves with wisdom, fortify our resolve, and chart a course toward debt reduction and ultimate liberation. So, gather 'round, my friends, and let us face this formidable foe with courage and determination.

The Chains of Debt - A Burden to Bear

Imagine, if you will, that you're a valiant knight, facing down the fearsome debt dragon that lurks in the shadows. Debt can feel like heavy chains, weighing us down and impeding our progress toward our dreams. Whether it's credit card debt, student loans, or a mortgage, each debt represents a link in the chain that binds us to financial servitude. But fear not, with knowledge and perseverance, we can break free from these chains and reclaim our financial sovereignty.

Know Thy Enemy - Understanding Your Debt

The first step in defeating the debt dragon is to understand the nature of your foe. Take stock of your debts – their types, amounts, and interest rates. Create a debt inventory, listing each debt from smallest to largest, regardless of interest rate. This will serve as your treasure map, guiding you in your quest for debt reduction. Knowledge is power, and by understanding your debts, you empower yourself to conquer them.

Choose Your Weapons Wisely - Strategies for Success

Armed with your treasure map, it's time to choose your weapons wisely. There are several strategies for debt reduction, each with its own strengths and advantages. The debt snowball method involves paying off debts from smallest to largest, gaining momentum as you slay each foe. The debt avalanche method prioritizes debts with the highest interest rates, saving you more gold in the long run. Whichever strategy you choose, wield it with determination and focus.

Slash and Burn - Cutting Expenses and Boosting Income

As you set sail on your quest for debt reduction, it's time to unleash the power of the slash-and-burn technique. Look for ways to slash unnecessary expenses from your budget, freeing up more gold to put toward debt repayment. Cut back on non-essential expenditures, such as dining out or entertainment, and redirect those doubloons toward your debt. And don't forget to seek out new sources of income – whether through a side hustle, freelancing, or investing in your skills. Every extra piece of gold you earn is a blow against the debt dragon.

Negotiate for Parley - Seeking Terms of Surrender

Don't hesitate to parley with your creditors in search of a truce. Reach out to your lenders and negotiate for lower interest rates, extended repayment terms, or even debt settlement agreements. Many creditors are willing to work with you to find a solution that benefits both parties, especially if it means avoiding default. But remember, negotiation requires diplomacy and tact – approach your creditors with respect and honesty.

Stay the Course - Persistence in the Face of Adversity

The journey to debt freedom may be fraught with challenges, but with courage and perseverance, we can overcome any obstacle in our path. Stay the course, even when the debt dragon breathes fire in your direction, and trust in the power of consistency and determination to see you through. Every small victory along the way – every debt repaid; every interest saved - brings you closer to financial liberation.

As you sail toward the shores of debt freedom, know that victory is within reach. With every debt repaid, you're breaking free from the chains that bind you and reclaiming your rightful place as the master of your financial destiny. So, muster your courage, sharpen your swords, and let the battle for debt reduction begin.

Chapter 8
Maximizing Your Savings Potential

In this chapter, we're setting sail on a grand expedition to uncover the mysteries of the millionaire code – the ancient cypher that holds the secrets to boundless wealth and abundance. Join me as we delve deep into the labyrinth of financial knowledge, uncovering hidden truths and unlocking the door to financial prosperity. So, gather 'round, my friends, and let us embark on this epic quest together.

The Quest for Prosperity

Imagine, if you will, that you're a bold explorer, venturing into uncharted waters in search of treasure beyond measure. The quest for prosperity is like a grand adventure – full of excitement, challenges, and the promise of untold riches. But amidst the vast ocean of financial opportunity lies a hidden treasure map – the millionaire code – waiting to be discovered by those brave enough to seek it out. Are you ready to embark on this epic quest and unlock the secrets of financial prosperity?

Cracking the Cipher

The first step in unravelling the millionaire code is to understand its foundational principles. At its core, the millionaire code is built upon timeless wisdom and universal truths that govern the creation and preservation of wealth. These principles include living below your means, investing wisely, diversifying your income streams, and giving back to others. By aligning your actions with these principles, you unlock the power of the millionaire code and set sail toward financial prosperity.

Living Below Your Means

One of the key secrets encoded within the millionaire code is the practice of living below your means. This means spending less than you earn and resisting the siren call of extravagant living. By embracing frugality and practising mindful spending, you free up more doubloons to put toward savings and investments, accelerating your journey toward financial independence. Remember, it's not about how much you earn – it's about how much you keep.

Investing Wisely

Another vital component of the millionaire code is the art of investing wisely. Instead of letting your doubloons sit idle, put them to work for you by investing in assets that have the potential to grow over time. Whether it's stocks, bonds, real estate, or business ventures, make your doubloons work as hard as you do. And don't forget to diversify your investments to spread your risk and maximize your potential returns.

Diversifying Your Income Streams

A key strategy encoded within the millionaire code is the practice of diversifying your income streams. Relying solely on a single source of income is like sailing a ship with only one sail – risky and vulnerable to storms. Instead, harness the power of multiple income streams – from your primary job to side hustles, investments, and passive income sources. By diversifying your income, you create a sturdy financial ship that can weather any storm.

Giving Back to Others

As you navigate the seas of financial prosperity, remember to give back to others along the way. Generosity is a cornerstone of the millionaire code – a principle that not only enriches the lives of others but also brings abundance and fulfilment to your own life. Whether it's through charitable donations, volunteering your time and talents, or mentoring others on their journey to success, find ways to give back and make a positive impact on the world around you. As you set sail on your quest to decode the millionaire code, remember that the journey itself is as important as the destination. Embrace the spirit of adventure, remain open to new opportunities, and never lose sight of your ultimate goal – financial prosperity and abundance. By following the principles of the millionaire code – living below your means, investing wisely, diversifying your income streams, and giving back to others – you unlock the secrets of wealth creation and chart a course toward a brighter future.

Chapter 9
Harnessing the Power of Compound Interest

In this chapter, we embark on a grand expedition into the enchanting realm of compound interest – a force so mighty, it can turn modest investments into vast fortunes over time. Join me as we navigate the intricate waters of financial knowledge, unlocking the secrets of compound interest and harnessing its boundless power to propel us toward financial freedom.

The Enigma of Compound Interest

Picture yourself as a seasoned mariner, navigating the boundless ocean of financial opportunity. Among the treasures that lie beneath the waves, none hold as much allure or mystery as compound interest. At its core, compound interest is a marvel of mathematics – the interest earned on an investment or savings is reinvested, generating even more interest over time. But beyond its mathematical elegance lies a profound truth – the ability of compound interest to amplify the growth of wealth, turning small investments into substantial fortunes with patience and persistence.

The Miracle of Time

The true magic of compound interest lies in its symbiotic relationship with time. The earlier you embark on your investment journey; the more time compound interest has to work its wonders. By starting early, you unleash the full potential of compound interest, allowing your investments to grow exponentially over the years. This is why savvy investors often say that time is their greatest asset – because with time, even the smallest investments can blossom into substantial wealth.

The Rule of 72

One of the most powerful tools in your arsenal for understanding compound interest is the legendary rule of 72. This simple rule allows you to estimate how long it will take for your investments to double in value at a given interest rate. Simply divide 72 by the annual interest rate, and you'll have an approximate number of years it will take for your investment to double. Armed with this knowledge, you can make informed decisions about where to invest your doubloons and maximize the power of compound interest.

The Magic of Consistency

Another key ingredient in unlocking the magic of compound interest is consistency. By making regular contributions to your investments or savings, you create a steady stream of capital that compounds over time. Whether it's through a regular investment plan, automated contributions to your retirement account, or simply setting aside a portion of your earnings each month, consistency is the secret sauce that turbocharges the power of compound interest and accelerates your journey toward financial independence.

The Power of Reinvestment

As your investments grow and compound over time, the power of compound interest only grows stronger. But to truly unleash its magic, you must reinvest the interest and dividends you earn back into your investments, allowing them to compound even further. This creates a snowball effect, where your wealth grows exponentially with each passing year. So, resist the temptation to spend your investment earnings and instead reinvest them to maximize the power of compound interest.

The Long-Term Perspective

The journey to financial freedom is a lifelong voyage, and compound interest is your steadfast companion along the way. By taking a long-term perspective and remaining patient and disciplined in your investment approach, you can unlock the full potential of compound interest and build a treasure trove of wealth that will sustain you for generations to come.

As you navigate the seas of financial prosperity, remember that compound interest is the wind in your sails – propelling you toward a future of unlimited opportunity and abundance. By starting early, remaining consistent, and reinvesting your earnings, you can unlock the full potential of compound interest and set sail toward a life of financial freedom and fulfilment.

Chapter 10

Strategic Tax
Planning for Wealth Growth

A crucial aspect of wealth building that can significantly impact your journey to financial freedom. In this chapter, we'll embark on a voyage through the complex waters of tax strategy, uncovering hidden treasures and powerful tactics to minimize taxes and maximize wealth growth. So, grab your compass and join me as we set sail on this epic quest for financial mastery.

The Tax Landscape

Imagine yourself as a seasoned navigator, steering your ship through the ever-shifting currents of the tax landscape. Taxes are a fundamental part of the financial seascape, but within their depths lie hidden opportunities to navigate more efficiently and keep more of your hard-earned treasure. By understanding the intricacies of the tax code and strategically planning your tax strategy, you can chart a course toward greater wealth and prosperity.

Know Your Tax Liabilities

The first step in strategic tax planning is to know your tax liabilities like the back of your hand. Dive deep into the depths of the tax code and familiarize yourself with the various taxes that may apply to you – from income taxes to capital gains taxes to property taxes and beyond. Understand how each tax is calculated and explore the deductions, credits, and loopholes that may help you navigate these treacherous waters with ease.

Maximize Retirement Contributions

One of the most powerful tools in your treasure chest for minimizing taxes is to maximize your contributions to retirement accounts. Contributions to traditional retirement accounts such as 401(k)s and IRAs are like hidden gems – they offer immediate tax benefits by reducing your taxable income and allowing your treasure to grow tax-deferred until you're ready to plunder it in retirement. So, hoist the Jolly Roger and make it a priority to stash as much treasure as you can in these tax-advantaged accounts.

Utilize Tax-Advantaged Investments

Another secret weapon in your arsenal for minimizing taxes is to invest in tax-advantaged vehicles that can shield your treasure from the taxman's grasp. Municipal bonds, Roth IRAs, and health savings accounts (HSAs) are like buried treasure waiting to be discovered – they offer tax benefits that can help your wealth grow more rapidly and securely. By strategically allocating your treasure to these tax-advantaged investments, you can sail smoother waters and keep more of your treasure for yourself.

Consider Tax-Loss Harvesting

In the world of investing, there's a strategy known as tax-loss harvesting that can help you turn a loss into a gain – or at least soften the blow. When the market turns against you and your investments decline in value, seize the opportunity to sell them at a loss and offset gains from other investments. This allows you to reduce your tax liability and keep more of your treasure in your chest where it belongs. So, keep a weather eye on the market and be ready to harvest tax losses when the time is right.

Plan for Charitable Giving

Charitable giving isn't just a noble pursuit – it's also a savvy tax strategy that can help you minimize your tax burden while making a positive impact on the world. Donations to qualified charitable organizations are like buried treasure waiting to be unearthed – they offer immediate tax benefits in the form of deductions that can lower your taxable income and reduce your tax bill. So, consider incorporating charitable giving into your tax planning strategy and watch your treasure grow while making a difference in the lives of others.

As you navigate the tax seas, remember that you don't have to go it alone. The tax code is like a maze of hidden passageways and secret chambers – and navigating it successfully requires expertise and knowledge. So, don't hesitate to seek out the guidance of qualified tax professionals such as accountants, tax attorneys, or financial advisors who can help you chart a course through these treacherous waters. By enlisting the help of experts, you can navigate the tax seas with confidence and set sail toward greater wealth and prosperity.

Chapter 11
Creating and Following
a Long-Term Investment Plan

In this chapter, we embark on an odyssey through the intricate waters of long-term investment planning – a vital compass point on the map to wealth creation and financial freedom. Join me as we unfurl the sails of opportunity and navigate the vast expanse of investment strategy, uncovering the secrets to crafting a robust and enduring plan for financial prosperity.

The Journey Begins

Close your eyes and envision yourself as the captain of your financial vessel, setting sail toward the horizon of wealth and abundance. Every great odyssey begins with a clear destination in mind. Likewise, your journey to financial independence starts with a meticulously crafted investment plan – a blueprint that will guide your course through the tumultuous seas of the financial world. By defining your objectives and charting a path toward your goals, you lay the groundwork for a prosperous and fulfilling future.

Setting Your Sails

The first order of business in crafting your investment plan is to hoist your sails and set your sights on the distant shores of financial success. Take stock of your dreams and aspirations – whether it's building a comfortable retirement nest egg, securing a home for your family, or creating a legacy for future generations. With clear and tangible goals in mind, you imbue your journey with purpose and direction, ensuring that every wave you ride brings you closer to your destination.

Navigating the Seas of Risk

As we journey onward, we must navigate the perilous waters of risk – a constant companion on the voyage to financial independence. The markets are a tempestuous sea, subject to the whims of fortune and the caprices of fate. Yet, with a well-crafted investment plan as our guiding star, we can weather any storm that comes our way. By diversifying our investments, balancing risk and reward, and staying true to our long-term vision, we chart a course that steers clear of danger and leads us toward calmer waters.

Choosing Your Crew

No captain sails alone, and neither should you. Surround yourself with a crew of trusted advisors and seasoned professionals who can help navigate the complexities of the investment landscape. Seek out wise counsel from financial planners, investment advisors, and tax experts who can offer guidance and support as you chart your course toward financial independence. With a knowledgeable crew by your side, you can navigate the treacherous waters of the financial world with confidence and clarity.

Staying the Course

In the face of uncertainty and adversity, it's essential to stay the course and remain steadfast in our commitment to our long-term investment plan. The journey to financial independence is not a sprint but a marathon – requiring patience, perseverance, and unwavering resolve. Though the winds may change, and the tides may turn, we must hold fast to our vision and trust in the wisdom of our plan. By staying focused on our goals and resisting the urge to veer off course, we ensure that every step we take brings us closer to our destination.

Reviewing Your Charts

As we sail onward, it's crucial to periodically review our charts and reassess our course to ensure we stay on track toward our goals. Take stock of your progress, evaluate your investment performance, and make any necessary adjustments to your plan to adapt to changing circumstances. By remaining vigilant and proactive, we can navigate the ever-changing currents of the financial markets with confidence and agility, ensuring that our journey remains true to our vision.

Along the journey to financial independence, it's essential to celebrate the victories – both big and small – that mark our progress along the way. Each milestone we reach is a testament to our dedication, determination, and resilience in the face of adversity. So, raise your flag high and toast to your success, knowing that every triumph brings us one step closer to the shores of financial freedom.

Chapter 12
Mastering the Psychology of Money

In this chapter, we embark on a profound exploration into the depths of the human psyche and unravel the intricate tapestry of beliefs, attitudes, and behaviours that shape our relationship with money. Join me as we navigate the uncharted waters of the mind and unlock the secrets to mastering the mindset of wealth – a journey that will empower you to chart your course toward financial freedom and abundance.

The Power of Belief

Imagine yourself as the captain of a magnificent vessel, navigating the vast ocean of opportunity. At the helm of every successful voyage lies a powerful belief – a deep-seated conviction in your ability to shape your own destiny and create the life of your dreams. Your beliefs about money, success, and abundance are like the sails that propel your ship forward – they determine the direction of your journey and the destinations you reach. So, cultivate a mindset of unwavering belief in your ability to achieve greatness, and watch as the universe conspires to fulfil your desires.

Conquering the Scarcity Mentality

One of the greatest challenges we face on the journey to financial mastery is overcoming the scarcity mentality – the belief that there is never enough to go around, and that success is reserved for the lucky few. But in reality, the universe is abundant, and there is more than enough wealth and opportunity to go around for everyone. By shifting your mindset from scarcity to abundance, you open yourself up to a world of limitless possibilities and unlock the door to unlimited prosperity.

Embracing Risk and Uncertainty

As we navigate the seas of wealth building, we must come to terms with the inherent risks and uncertainties that accompany the journey. The fear of failure and the unknown can often hold us back from taking bold action and seizing the opportunities that lie before us. However, true wealth is built on the foundation of risk and uncertainty – it is the willingness to step outside our comfort zones and embrace the unknown that ultimately leads to success. So, hoist the anchor and set sail into uncharted waters, knowing that fortune favours the bold.

Fostering Patience and Discipline

In the fast-paced world of finance, patience and discipline are your most valuable assets. The journey to financial independence is not a sprint but a marathon – it requires steadfast resolve and unwavering commitment to your goals. Resist the temptation to chase after quick riches or succumb to the allure of get-rich-quick schemes. Instead, focus on the long-term and stay the course, knowing that slow and steady wins the race in the end.

Mastery of Delayed Gratification

One of the hallmarks of financial mastery is the ability to delay gratification – to forgo short-term pleasures in exchange for long-term rewards. Whether it's resisting the urge to indulge in unnecessary luxuries or sacrificing immediate pleasures for future gains, mastering the art of delayed gratification is essential for building wealth and achieving financial independence. So, practice patience and discipline in all your financial endeavours, knowing that the rewards will be well worth the wait.

Adopting a Growth Mindset

In the ever-evolving world of finance, a growth mindset is your most powerful ally. Instead of viewing challenges as insurmountable obstacles, see them as opportunities for growth and learning. Embrace failure as a stepping stone to success and approach every setback as a chance to refine your skills and strategies. With a growth mindset as your compass, there's no limit to what you can achieve on your journey to financial mastery.

As you navigate the seas of wealth-building and master the psychology of money, take time to celebrate your victories along the way. Each milestone you reach – whether it's overcoming a limiting belief, achieving a financial goal, or mastering a new skill – is a testament to your courage, resilience, and determination. So, raise your flag high and toast to your success, knowing that every triumph brings you one step closer to the shores of financial freedom.

Chapter 13
Navigating Market Volatility with Confidence

In this chapter, we're embarking on a voyage through the tempestuous waters of market volatility – a natural phenomenon that can strike fear into the hearts of even the most seasoned investors. But fear not, for with the right mindset and strategy, you can navigate these choppy waters with confidence and emerge stronger and more resilient than ever before. So, hoist the mainsail and prepare to chart a course through the stormy seas of market volatility.

Understanding the Nature of Volatility

Picture yourself as the captain of a sturdy vessel, navigating the unpredictable currents of the market. Market volatility is like a sudden squall – it can appear out of nowhere and toss your portfolio to and for with wild abandon. But volatility is not the enemy – it's simply a natural part of the ebb and flow of the market. By understanding the nature of volatility and accepting it as a normal aspect of investing, you can approach market fluctuations with calmness and confidence.

Staying True to Your Course

The key to navigating market volatility is to stay true to your course and resist the temptation to react impulsively to short-term fluctuations. Remember that investing is a long-term endeavour, and short-term market movements are nothing more than noise. Instead of trying to time the market or chase after hot stocks, focus on your long-term goals and stick to your investment plan. By maintaining a steady hand and staying disciplined in the face of volatility, you can weather any storm that comes your way.

Diversifying Your Holdings

One of the most effective strategies for navigating market volatility is to diversify your holdings across a variety of asset classes and investment vehicles. Just as a ship is safer when it has multiple sails to catch the wind, your portfolio is more resilient when it's spread across different types of investments. By diversifying your holdings, you can reduce the risk of large losses from any single investment and cushion the impact of market downturns on your overall portfolio.

Capitalizing on Opportunities

While market volatility can be unsettling, it also presents opportunities for savvy investors to capitalize on mispricing's and inefficiencies in the market. Instead of viewing volatility as a threat, see it as a chance to scoop up high-quality assets at discounted prices. Keep a watchful eye on the market and be prepared to pounce when opportunities arise. By maintaining a contrarian mindset and buying when others are selling, you can turn market volatility to your advantage and enhance your long-term returns.

Keeping Emotions in Check

One of the biggest challenges in navigating market volatility is keeping your emotions in check. Fear and greed are powerful emotions that can cloud your judgment and lead to irrational decision-making. Instead of succumbing to panic or euphoria, stay calm and rational in the face of market fluctuations. Trust in your investment plan and stick to your predetermined strategy, knowing that staying disciplined in turbulent times is the key to long-term success.

Seeking Wisdom from Seasoned Mariners

As you navigate the seas of market volatility, don't hesitate to seek wisdom and guidance from seasoned mariners who have weathered their fair share of storms. Learn from their experiences and heed their advice on how to navigate choppy waters with confidence and grace. Whether it's seeking out the counsel of financial advisors, reading the insights of seasoned investors, or participating in investment forums and communities, surround yourself with a network of trusted advisors who can help guide you through turbulent times.

In the face of market volatility, it's essential to remain resilient and steadfast in your commitment to your long-term goals. Remember that every storm eventually passes, and brighter days lie ahead on the horizon. By maintaining a positive attitude and staying focused on your journey toward financial independence, you can navigate even the roughest seas with confidence and emerge stronger and more resilient than ever before.

Chapter 14
Networking and Building Wealth-Oriented Relationships

In this chapter, we embark on a journey into the realm of networking and relationship building – a crucial aspect of wealth creation that often goes overlooked. Join me as we cast our nets wide and explore the seas of opportunity, forging connections and alliances that will propel us toward financial abundance and prosperity.

The Power of Your Network

Picture yourself as the captain of a grand fleet, navigating the vast ocean of opportunity. Your network is like a fleet of ships – each connection representing a potential opportunity or resource that can help you achieve your goals. Whether it's finding new business opportunities, gaining access to valuable information, or receiving mentorship and guidance, your network is an invaluable asset on your journey to financial success.

Cultivating Wealth-Oriented Relationships

One of the keys to building wealth is surrounding yourself with like-minded individuals who share your goals and aspirations. Seek out relationships with people who are wealth-oriented – those who are ambitious, entrepreneurial, and forward-thinking. By surrounding yourself with individuals who are on a similar path to success, you create a supportive environment that fosters growth, innovation, and collaboration.

Adding Value to Your Network

Networking is not just about what you can get – it's also about what you can give. Look for opportunities to add value to your network by offering assistance, support, and expertise to those around you. Whether it's providing a helping hand to a fellow entrepreneur, sharing valuable insights and information, or making introductions to valuable contacts, find ways to contribute to the success of others. By giving generously to your network, you sow the seeds of reciprocity and build goodwill that will pay dividends in the future.

Expanding Your Horizons

Don't limit yourself to networking within your immediate circle – cast your net far and wide to connect with individuals from diverse backgrounds and industries. Attend networking events, join professional organizations, and participate in online communities and forums to expand your reach and connect with people who can offer new perspectives and opportunities. By broadening your horizons and diversifying your network, you increase your chances of stumbling upon valuable connections and opportunities that can accelerate your journey to financial success.

Building Trust and Rapport

Trust is the currency of relationships, and building strong, genuine connections is essential for cultivating lasting relationships that endure the test of time. Be authentic, transparent, and reliable in your interactions with others, and strive to establish rapport based on mutual respect and shared values. By nurturing trust and credibility within your network, you create a foundation of support and cooperation that will serve you well on your quest for wealth and abundance.

Seeking Mentorship and Guidance

As you navigate the seas of wealth creation, don't hesitate to seek out mentorship and guidance from those who have sailed these waters before you. A mentor is like a seasoned navigator who can offer valuable insights, advice, and wisdom to help you navigate the challenges and opportunities of wealth building. Look for mentors who have achieved the level of success you aspire to and who are willing to share their knowledge and experience with you. By learning from the best and standing on the shoulders of giants, you can accelerate your journey to financial success and avoid common pitfalls along the way.

Building wealth-oriented relationships is not a one-time endeavour – it's an ongoing journey that requires patience, persistence, and nurturing. Take the time to cultivate and strengthen your relationships over time, investing in the long-term success and prosperity of your network. Stay in touch with your contacts, follow up on commitments, and look for ways to continue adding value and support to those around you. By nurturing your relationships with care and intentionality, you create a network of allies and advocates who will stand by your side through thick and thin, helping you achieve your goals and dreams.

Chapter 15
Leveraging Technology for Financial Management

In this chapter, we delve into the world of technology and explore how it can be harnessed to streamline and optimize your financial management practices. Join me as we embark on a journey through the digital landscape, uncovering the tools and techniques that will revolutionize the way you manage your money and propel you toward financial abundance and prosperity. So, hoist the sails and prepare to set forth on a voyage of technological enlightenment.

The Digital Revolution

Imagine yourself as the captain of a sleek, high-tech vessel, navigating the digital seas of the 21st century. We are living in an age of unprecedented technological innovation, where smartphones, computers, and the internet have transformed every aspect of our lives – including how we manage our finances. From online banking and budgeting apps to investment platforms and robot advisors, technology has opened up a world of possibilities for optimizing our financial management practices and achieving greater control over our money.

Streamlining Financial Transactions

One of the most significant benefits of technology is its ability to streamline financial transactions and eliminate the need for cumbersome paperwork and manual processes. With online banking and payment apps, you can manage your accounts, transfer funds, pay bills, and track expenses with just a few taps on your smartphone or clicks of your mouse. Say goodbye to long lines at the bank and piles of paper statements – technology puts the power of financial management right at your fingertips.

Automating Savings and Investing

Another advantage of technology is its ability to automate savings and investing, making it easier than ever to build wealth over time. With automatic transfers and recurring contributions, you can effortlessly funnel a portion of your income into savings accounts, retirement accounts, or investment portfolios without having to lift a finger. By harnessing the power of automation, you can take the guesswork out of saving and investing and ensure that your money is working hard for you around the clock.

Utilizing Financial Management Apps

There's a treasure trove of financial management apps available today that can help you take control of your finances and make informed decisions about your money. Whether it's budgeting apps like Mint or YNAB, investment platforms like Robinhood or Acorns, or personal finance apps like Personal Capital or Quicken, there's an app for every aspect of financial management. Explore the app store and find the tools that best suit your needs and preferences and watch as technology transforms the way you manage your money for the better.

Harnessing Data Analytics

With the advent of big data and analytics, technology has given us unprecedented insights into our financial behaviour and habits. By leveraging data analytics tools and platforms, you can gain valuable insights into your spending patterns, investment performance, and overall financial health. Armed with this knowledge, you can make more informed decisions about your money and identify areas for improvement that will help you achieve your financial goals faster and more efficiently.

Protecting Your Digital Assets

As you navigate the digital seas of financial management, it's essential to take steps to protect your digital assets from cyber threats and security breaches. From identity theft and fraud to data breaches and hacking attacks, the digital world is fraught with dangers that can jeopardize your financial security. Be vigilant about cybersecurity best practices, such as using strong passwords, enabling two-factor authentication, and regularly updating your software and antivirus programs. By taking proactive steps to safeguard your digital assets, you can navigate the digital landscape with confidence and peace of mind.

As technology continues to evolve and transform the world of finance, it's essential to embrace a mindset of continuous learning and innovation. Stay curious and open-minded about new technologies and trends in financial management and be willing to adapt and evolve your strategies as the digital landscape evolves. By staying ahead of the curve and harnessing the power of technology to its fullest potential, you can navigate the digital seas of financial management with confidence and precision, charting a course toward greater wealth and prosperity.

Chapter 16
Protecting Your Assets:
Insurance and Estate Planning

In this chapter, we dive into the crucial realm of asset protection through insurance and estate planning. Just as a wise captain safeguards their ship from storms and pirates, it's essential to protect your hard-earned wealth from unforeseen risks and ensure a smooth transfer of assets to future generations. Join me as we explore the strategies and techniques that will fortify your financial fortress and safeguard your treasure for generations to come.

The Pillars of Asset Protection

Picture yourself as the guardian of a great treasure, entrusted with its safekeeping and preservation. Asset protection is the cornerstone of financial security – it's the armour that shields your wealth from the perils of life's uncertainties. Insurance and estate planning are the twin pillars of asset protection, providing a robust framework for safeguarding your assets and ensuring their preservation for future generations. By fortifying your financial fortress with these essential tools, you can sleep soundly knowing that your treasure is safe from harm.

Navigating the Seas of Risk

Life is full of risks – from accidents and illnesses to natural disasters and lawsuits, there are countless threats that can jeopardize your financial security. Insurance is your first line of defence against these risks, providing financial protection and peace of mind in the face of life's uncertainties. Whether it's health insurance, life insurance, property insurance, or liability insurance, having the right coverage in place can shield you from financial ruin and ensure that you weather any storm that comes your way.

Choosing the Right Coverage

When it comes to insurance, one size does not fit all – it's essential to choose the right coverage that meets your specific needs and circumstances. Take the time to assess your risks and identify areas where insurance can provide valuable protection. Whether you're protecting your health, your home, your business, or your loved ones, make sure you have the right coverage in place to safeguard your assets and mitigate potential losses. Consult with a trusted insurance advisor to explore your options and find the coverage that best suits your needs and budget.

Building a Strong Estate Plan

In addition to insurance, estate planning is a critical component of asset protection that ensures the orderly transfer of your wealth to your heirs and beneficiaries. A well-crafted estate plan includes essential documents such as wills, trusts, powers of attorney, and healthcare directives, which provide instructions for the management and distribution of your assets in the event of your incapacity or death. By creating a comprehensive estate plan, you can protect your assets from probate, minimize estate taxes, and ensure that your wishes are carried out according to your wishes.

Protecting Your Legacy

Estate planning is not just about protecting your assets – it's also about preserving your legacy and ensuring that your values and beliefs endure for future generations. Take the time to consider the legacy you want to leave behind and create a plan that reflects your values and priorities. Whether it's passing on a family business, supporting charitable causes, or providing for the education and well-being of your loved ones, estate planning allows you to shape the future and leave a lasting impact on the world.

Reviewing and Updating Your Plan

As you journey through life, it's essential to periodically review and update your insurance and estate plan to ensure that it remains aligned with your goals and circumstances. Life is full of changes – from marriage and divorce to births and deaths, your life circumstances can change in an instant. By regularly reviewing your plan and making necessary adjustments, you can adapt to changing circumstances and ensure that your asset protection strategy remains effective and up to date.

When it comes to insurance and estate planning, it's essential to seek professional guidance from trusted advisors who can help you navigate the complexities of asset protection and ensure that your plan is robust and effective. Consult with experienced insurance agents, estate planning attorneys, and financial advisors who can provide personalized advice and guidance tailored to your unique needs and circumstances. By enlisting the help of knowledgeable professionals, you can navigate the seas of asset protection with confidence and peace of mind, knowing that your treasure is safe and secure.

Chapter 17
Evaluating and Seizing Entrepreneurial Opportunities

In this chapter, we embark on a thrilling voyage into the world of entrepreneurship – a realm of boundless opportunity and unlimited potential for those brave enough to seize the helm and chart their own course. Join me as we set forth on a journey of discovery, exploring the strategies and techniques for evaluating and seizing entrepreneurial opportunities that can lead to untold riches and success beyond your wildest dreams.

The Call of the Entrepreneur

Picture yourself as the captain of a mighty vessel, sailing the seas of commerce in search of treasure and adventure. The entrepreneurial spirit is the lifeblood of innovation and progress – it's the driving force behind every great endeavour and the spark that ignites the flames of creativity and ambition. Whether you're launching a new business, inventing a revolutionary product, or pioneering a groundbreaking service, entrepreneurship is the ultimate expression of human ingenuity and resourcefulness.

Spotting Opportunity on the Horizon

In the vast ocean of possibilities, entrepreneurial opportunities abound for those with the vision to spot them. Keep a keen eye on the horizon and remain vigilant for signs of opportunity – whether it's a gap in the market, an unmet need, or a problem in search of a solution. Opportunities often present themselves in unexpected ways, so stay open-minded and receptive to new ideas and possibilities. By cultivating a mindset of curiosity and exploration, you can uncover hidden gems that others overlook and seize the opportunity to create value and wealth.

Evaluating Risk and Reward

Every entrepreneurial opportunity comes with its own set of risks and rewards – it's essential to carefully evaluate the potential risks and rewards before setting sail. Conduct thorough market research, assess the competitive landscape, and crunch the numbers to determine the feasibility and profitability of your venture. Consider factors such as market demand, competition, scalability, and financial viability when evaluating entrepreneurial opportunities. By conducting due diligence and weighing the risks and rewards, you can make informed decisions that maximize your chances of success and minimize your exposure to potential pitfalls.

Taking Calculated Risks

Entrepreneurship is not for the faint of heart – it requires a willingness to take calculated risks and venture into uncharted territory in pursuit of your goals. While it's essential to assess and mitigate risks to the extent possible, it's also important to recognize that risk is an inherent part of the entrepreneurial journey. Embrace uncertainty and ambiguity with courage and confidence, knowing that every risk you take is an opportunity for growth and learning. By taking calculated risks and stepping outside your comfort zone, you can unlock new opportunities and achieve greater success than you ever thought possible.

Seizing the Moment

Opportunities rarely come knocking twice – it's essential to act decisively and seize the opportunity when it presents itself. Don't let fear or hesitation hold you back from pursuing your dreams – trust your instincts and take bold action in pursuit of your goals. Whether it's launching a new business, pursuing a partnership, or investing in a promising opportunity, seize the moment with courage and conviction, knowing that fortune favours the bold.

Adapting and Innovating

In the ever-changing seas of entrepreneurship, adaptability and innovation are your most valuable allies. Stay agile and responsive to changes in the market and be willing to pivot and adapt your strategy as needed. Embrace failure as a natural part of the entrepreneurial journey and use it as an opportunity to learn, grow, and evolve. By continually innovating and refining your approach, you can stay ahead of the competition and position yourself for long-term success in the dynamic world of entrepreneurship.

As you navigate the seas of entrepreneurship, don't hesitate to seek out mentorship and guidance from those who have sailed these waters before you. A mentor is like a seasoned navigator who can offer valuable insights, advice, and wisdom to help you navigate the challenges and opportunities of entrepreneurship. Seek out mentors who have achieved the level of success you aspire to and who are willing to share their knowledge and experience with you. By learning from the best and standing on the shoulders of giants, you can accelerate your journey to entrepreneurial success and avoid common pitfalls along the way.

Chapter 18
Scaling Your
Business for Profitability

In this chapter, we set sail on a thrilling expedition into the realm of business growth and expansion – a journey that promises untold riches and boundless opportunities for those bold enough to hoist the Jolly Roger and set forth on the high seas of commerce. Join me as we explore the strategies and tactics for scaling your business for profitability, transforming your humble vessel into a mighty flagship that dominates the market and reaps bountiful rewards.

The Quest for Growth

Picture yourself as the captain of a small ship, sailing the seas of commerce in search of treasure and adventure. Every entrepreneur dreams of building a business that not only survives but thrives – a business that grows and expands, leaving a lasting legacy of success and prosperity. Scaling your business for profitability is the ultimate quest – it's the pursuit of growth and expansion that unlocks the full potential of your enterprise and paves the way for untold riches and abundance.

Setting Sail for Success

Scaling your business requires a strategic approach and careful planning to ensure that your vessel remains seaworthy as it navigates the treacherous waters of growth. Start by defining your vision and goals for growth – where do you see your business in five years, ten years, or even twenty years? Identify opportunities for expansion and diversification that align with your long-term vision and values. Whether it's expanding into new markets, launching new products or services, or acquiring complementary businesses, set sail for success with a clear plan and a bold vision for the future.

Navigating the Challenges of Growth

Scaling your business is not without its challenges – from resource constraints and operational inefficiencies to market saturation and competition, there are countless obstacles that can impede your progress. It's essential to anticipate and navigate these challenges with skill and finesse, adjusting your course as needed to stay on course toward your goals. Keep a close eye on your finances, streamline your operations, and invest in the resources and infrastructure needed to support growth. By navigating the challenges of growth with agility and resilience, you can overcome any obstacle that stands in your way and emerge stronger and more profitable than ever before.

Expanding Your Crew

As your business grows, so too must your crew – it's essential to assemble a team of skilled and dedicated individuals who can help you navigate the seas of expansion and achieve your goals. Surround yourself with talented professionals who share your vision and values and empower them to take ownership of their roles and contribute to the success of the enterprise. Invest in training and development programs to help your crew members grow and evolve with the business and foster a culture of collaboration and innovation that encourages creativity and excellence. By expanding your crew and harnessing the collective talents and expertise of your team, you can propel your business to new heights of success and profitability.

Leveraging Technology and Innovation

In the digital age, technology and innovation are the wind in your sails – they can propel your business forward with speed and efficiency, enabling you to scale with greater ease and agility. Invest in technology solutions that streamline your operations, improve productivity, and enhance the customer experience. Whether it's implementing cloud-based software, leveraging data analytics, or embracing automation and artificial intelligence, harness the power of technology to fuel your growth and drive profitability.

Staying True to Your Values

As you scale your business for profitability, it's essential to stay true to your values and principles – they are the compass that guides your journey and keeps you on course toward your goals. Resist the temptation to sacrifice integrity for short-term gains or compromise your values in pursuit of profit. Instead, anchor your decisions and actions in your core values and ethics, and let them serve as a beacon of light that guides you through the stormy seas of business growth. By staying true to your values, you can build a business that not only succeeds financially but also makes a positive impact on the world.

As you navigate the seas of business growth and scale your enterprise for profitability, take time to celebrate your successes along the way. Whether it's reaching a major milestone, achieving a significant revenue goal, or conquering a formidable challenge, every victory is a cause for celebration. Share your successes with your crew and stakeholders and take pride in the progress you've made on your journey toward entrepreneurial success and financial prosperity.

Chapter 19
Balancing Risk and Reward in Your Investment Portfolio

In this chapter, we embark on a voyage into the tumultuous waters of investment, where the winds of risk and reward blow strong and true. Join me as we navigate the tides of uncertainty, charting a course toward financial prosperity by striking the delicate balance between risk and reward in your investment portfolio.

The Art of Investing

Picture yourself as the captain of a grand vessel, navigating the vast ocean of investment opportunities in search of treasure and fortune. Investing is both an art and a science – it requires skill, knowledge, and intuition to navigate the complexities of the market and achieve success. At its core, investing is about striking the right balance between risk and reward – maximizing your potential for returns while minimizing the likelihood of losses. By mastering the art of investing, you can unlock the door to financial freedom and abundance.

Understanding Risk and Reward

Risk and reward are the twin pillars of investing – they are inseparable companions that must be carefully balanced to achieve optimal results. Risk refers to the possibility of losing money or experiencing negative returns on your investments, while reward refers to the potential for earning profits and achieving positive returns. Every investment carries a certain degree of risk, but with risk comes the potential for reward. The key is to understand the relationship between risk and reward and strike a balance that aligns with your investment objectives, time horizon, and risk tolerance.

Assessing Your Risk Tolerance

Before setting sail on your investment journey, it's essential to assess your risk tolerance – your ability and willingness to tolerate fluctuations in the value of your investments. Are you comfortable with the possibility of losing money in pursuit of higher returns, or do you prefer to take a more conservative approach with lower risk and lower potential returns?

Understanding your risk

Tolerance is critical for constructing an investment portfolio that aligns with your goals and preferences. Take the time to evaluate your risk tolerance honestly and objectively and use it as a guide for selecting investments that are appropriate for your individual circumstances.

Diversification, your first mate

Diversification is your first mate on the voyage to balanced investing – it's the strategy of spreading your investments across a variety of asset classes, industries, and geographic regions to reduce the impact of any single investment on your overall portfolio. By diversifying your holdings, you can minimize the risk of significant losses from any one investment while maximizing the potential for returns from multiple sources. Whether it's stocks, bonds, real estate, or alternative investments, diversification allows you to sail with confidence, knowing that your portfolio is well-positioned to weather any storm that comes your way.

Managing Volatility and Market Fluctuations

Volatility is a natural part of the investment landscape – it's the ebb and flow of market fluctuations that can cause prices to rise and fall unpredictably.

While volatility can be unsettling, it also presents opportunities for savvy investors to capitalize on mispricing's and inefficiencies in the market. By staying disciplined and focused on your long-term goals, you can navigate market fluctuations with confidence and use them to your advantage.

Seeking Alpha

The Pursuit of Outperformance: In the quest for investment success, many investors seek alpha – the excess return earned above the market's expected return, often achieved through active management and skilful decision-making. Whether it's selecting individual stocks, timing the market, or employing alternative investment strategies, the pursuit of alpha is a noble endeavour that requires discipline, research, and a keen understanding of market dynamics. While alpha can offer the potential for higher returns, it also comes with increased risk and volatility. It's essential to weigh the potential benefits and drawbacks of seeking alpha and consider whether it aligns with your investment objectives and risk tolerance.

As you navigate the tides of investment, remember the importance of patience and discipline. Investing is a long-term journey, and success often requires the ability to stay the course and resist the temptation to react impulsively to short-term market fluctuations. Stick to your investment plan, maintain a diversified portfolio, and avoid making emotional decisions based on fear or greed. By staying patient and disciplined in the face of uncertainty, you can ride out the inevitable ups and downs of the market and achieve your long-term financial goals.

Chapter 20
Achieving Financial Freedom:
Review and Next Steps

In this final chapter, we unveil the secrets of millionaire success – the culmination of our journey through the seas of entrepreneurship, investing, and financial mastery. Join me as we delve into the treasure trove of wisdom and insight gleaned from our voyage, unlocking the keys to unlocking the gates of prosperity and achieving the ultimate dream of millionaire success.

The Quest for Wealth

Picture yourself as the captain of a magnificent galleon, sailing the seas of opportunity in search of treasure and fortune. The quest for wealth is the ultimate adventure – a journey of self-discovery, exploration, and mastery that leads to untold riches and abundance. Whether you're an aspiring entrepreneur, a seasoned investor, or a budding millionaire, the path to success begins with a clear vision, a bold plan, and an unwavering commitment to achieving your goals. Set sail with confidence and determination, knowing that the treasures of wealth and prosperity await those who dare to pursue their dreams.

The Mindset of Success

The first step on the path to millionaire success is mastering the mindset of success – it's the foundation upon which all great achievements are built. Cultivate a mindset of abundance, positivity, and possibility, and banish thoughts of scarcity, limitation, and doubt from your mind. Believe in yourself and your ability to achieve greatness, and let nothing stand in the way of your dreams. With the right mindset, you can overcome any obstacle, conquer any challenge, and manifest your deepest desires into reality.

The Power of Financial Education

Knowledge is power – especially when it comes to mastering the art of millionaire success. Educate yourself about the principles of finance, investing, and entrepreneurship, and arm yourself with the tools and strategies needed to navigate the seas of wealth with skill and confidence.

Read books, attend seminars, and seek out mentors who can offer valuable insights and guidance on your journey. The more you know, the better equipped you'll be to make informed decisions and seize opportunities for growth and prosperity.

Taking Action with Purpose

Action is the wind in your sails – it's what propels you forward on the journey to millionaire success. Take bold action toward your goals each day, and let nothing stand in the way of your progress. Whether it's launching a new business, investing in the stock market, or pursuing a lucrative opportunity, seize the moment with courage and conviction, knowing that fortune favours the bold. With each step you take, you move closer to realizing your dreams and achieving the ultimate prize of millionaire success.

Embracing Failure as a Stepping Stone

Along the journey to millionaire success, failure is inevitable – but it's also a valuable teacher and a stepping stone to greatness. Embrace failure as a natural part of the learning process, and use it as an opportunity to grow, learn, and evolve. Every setback is a lesson in disguise – it's an opportunity to refine your strategy, sharpen your skills, and emerge stronger and more resilient than ever before. Don't let fear of failure hold you back from pursuing your dreams – instead, embrace it as a necessary part of the journey to success.

Building Wealth for the Long Term

As you navigate the seas of wealth and prosperity, remember that true wealth is built for the long term. Avoid the temptation to seek quick fixes or pursue get-rich-quick schemes that promise easy riches with little effort. Instead, focus on building a solid foundation of wealth through disciplined saving, strategic investing, and prudent financial management. Set long-term goals and stay committed to your vision, knowing that patience, persistence, and perseverance are the keys to unlocking the gates of millionaire success.

As you achieve success and accumulate wealth, remember to pay it forward and share your blessings with others. Use your wealth and influence to make a positive impact on the world around you, whether it's through charitable giving, mentorship, or community service. Share your wisdom and insights with those who are following in your footsteps and be a beacon of light and inspiration for others on their journey to success. By sharing your wealth and wisdom with others, you not only enrich their lives but also create a legacy that will endure for generations to come.

Bringing everything into harmony

In the timeless journey encapsulated within the pages of "Path to Seven Figures Wealth Strategies," we embark on a transformative odyssey through the realms of financial empowerment. Much like seasoned navigators charting a course through uncharted waters, we delve deep into the intricacies of entrepreneurship, investing, and personal finance.

At its heart, this book is a beacon of hope and opportunity for those who dare to dream big and aspire to achieve the pinnacle of financial success – the coveted seven figures of wealth. But make no mistake; this journey is not for the faint of heart. It requires courage, determination, and a willingness to challenge the status quo in pursuit of greatness.

Our voyage begins with the foundational principles of financial mastery, where we learn to cultivate the mindset of abundance and possibility that is essential for success and we come to understand that true wealth is not merely measured in dollars and cents but in the mindset of abundance and the willingness to take calculated risks in pursuit of our dreams.

As we set sail into the vast ocean of entrepreneurship, we discover the art of spotting opportunities and seizing them with courage and conviction. We learn how to build businesses that generate passive income streams and create long-term wealth.

But the journey doesn't end there. With the power of investing, we unlock the secrets of building a diversified portfolio that can withstand the winds of market volatility and harness the forces of compound interest to grow our wealth exponentially.

Through strategic tax planning and savvy financial management, we learn to navigate the complexities of personal finance and minimize our tax liabilities while maximizing our returns.

And as we sail toward our destination, we never forget to share our wealth and wisdom with others, creating a ripple effect of prosperity that extends far beyond our own shores. For true wealth is not hoarded but shared, and it is through our acts of generosity and kindness that we leave a lasting legacy of abundance and prosperity for generations to come.

So, my fellow adventurers, heed the call of the sea and embark on the journey of a lifetime. With "Path to Seven Figures Wealth Strategies" as your guide, the possibilities are endless, and the rewards are boundless. May your journey be filled with success, fulfilment, and the sweet taste of seven-figure wealth.

www.ingramcontent.com/pod-product-compliance
Lightning Source LLC
Chambersburg PA
CBHW070921290526
45795CB00001B/375